My Devotional Journal

A spiritual journey
of prayer and
encouragement with
God's suffering people

Patrick Sookhdeo

My Devotional Journal

Published in the United States by Isaac Publishing

6729 Curran Street, McLean VA 22101

Copyright © 2010 Isaac Publishing

Produced by Barnabas Fund, which is known as Barnabas Aid in the USA

ISBN 978-0-9825218-2-3

Printed in the United Kingdom

"I would like to express my heartfelt thanks to the many colleagues and friends who have inspired this volume with their suggestions, their contributions and their practical assistance."

Patrick Sookhdeo

LIFE IS A JOURNEY

As Christians we plant our footsteps in those of our Lord and go wherever He leads us. Jesus' life led Him to the cross, the resurrection, the ascension and to glory itself. This too is the pattern for our lives.

We are led often to the cross. Pain and suffering are normal for the Christian, for we are not immune from the effects of the world, the conditions that surround us and our own human weaknesses. We experience bereavement, sickness and loss. But many Christians, in fact one in ten of all Christians, experience another set of difficulties – the suffering that comes as a result of their allegiance to Christ, the pain of rejection, the pressure of discrimination or injustice and violent persecution as they take up the cross of Christ. This can lead even to death.

In this journal, we will seek to journey with the suffering Church as they seek to follow in the footsteps of our Lord. We will look to empathise with their ordeals but also with them to experience something of the joy and the glory that often come with pain and suffering.

The Christian life should be one of joyful encounter, for Christ is alive. He is the hope of our calling, the goal of our lives. Whilst on earth, it was His joy that He bequeathed to His disciples despite walking the way of the cross. He gifted them that inner, overwhelming joy which only He could give. This joy transcends all human conditions and circumstances. It bridges every obstacle and crosses every valley. When we love our Lord and embrace the cross, it is then that we experience most fully His joy and His glory.

Dr Patrick Sookhdeo
International Director, Barnabas Fund/Barnabas Aid

"Taste and see that the LORD is good; blessed are those who take refuge in him."

Psalm 34:8

Drawing of a blind girl receiving her sight and praising God by **Nora Akram** (22), a Christian refugee who is deaf and mute, from Baghdad.

"I myself will see him with my own eyes – I, and not another. How my heart yearns within me!"

Job 19:27

JANUARY

"I consider everything a loss because of the surpassing worth of knowing Christ Jesus my Lord."   Philippians 3:8a

---

When the son of a prominent Hamas leader in the West Bank left Islam and became a Christian, he knew it meant leaving everything he knew and loved behind.

Masab Hassan Yousef, now called Joseph, described his feelings:

> Just stop and think for a minute about announcing your Christianity; you feel sick immediately because it's crazy. You're not just saying goodbye to a religion, to a tradition. You are saying goodbye to a culture, to a civilisation. Even the process of taking your skin off your bones might be easier than saying goodbye to your mother and to everybody, especially when you are a well-known figure in your society and everybody has high expectations that one day in the future you will be one of the leaders.
>
> Suddenly you are starting from scratch and cancelling everything you have. But when it started, I was ready for any circumstances. I thought about the worst conditions that could happen as consequences after my announcement. But – and I tell you this is a miracle, this is how God works – you carry the cross and rely on Him completely and He takes care of everything.

"Whoever wants to be my disciple must deny themselves
and take up their cross and follow me."   Mark 8:34b

"Be strong and courageous. Do not be afraid; do not be discouraged, for the LORD your God will be with you wherever you go."

Joshua 1:9b

Burundian convert to Christianity cries as she shares her testimony at a convert discipleship conference funded by Barnabas

"There are tears on my cheek, and oh! the heart is sad."
Fatima Al-Mutairi

10

Extracts from *And we for the sake of Christ all things bear*. This poem was written by Fatima Al-Mutairi, a 26-year-old Saudi Christian, shortly before she was martyred for her faith. She had her tongue cut out and was burnt to death, apparently by her brother, when her family found out that she had converted from Islam to Christianity.

"My comfort in my suffering is this: Your promise preserves my life."

Psalm 119:50

MAY the Lord Jesus guide you, O Muslims
And enlighten your hearts that you might love others
The forum does not revile the Master of the prophets
It is for the display of truth, and for you it was revealed
This is the truth that you do not know
What we profess are the words of the Master of the prophets
We do not worship the cross, and we are not possessed
We worship the Lord Jesus, the Light of the worlds
We followed Jesus Christ, the Clear Truth

...

We chose our way, the way of the rightly guided
And every man is free to choose any religion
Be content to leave us to ourselves to be believers in Jesus
Let us live in grace before our time comes
There are tears on my cheek, and oh! the heart is sad
To those who become Christians, you are so cruel!
And the Messiah says, "Blessed are the Persecuted"
And we for the sake of Christ all things bear
What is it to you that we are infidels?
You do not enter our graves, as if with us buried
Enough – your swords do not concern me, not evil nor disgrace
Your threats do not trouble me, and we are not afraid
And by God, I am unto death a Christian – Verily
I cry for what passed by, of a sad life
I was far from the Lord Jesus for many years
O History record! and bear witness, O witnesses!
We are Christians – in the path of Christ we tread
Take from me this word, and note it well
You see, Jesus is my Lord, and he is the Best of protectors
I advise you to pity yourself, to clap your hands in mourning
See your look of ugly hatred
Man is brother to man, Oh learned ones
Where is the humanity, the love, and where are you?
As to my last words, I pray to the Lord of the worlds
Jesus the Messiah, the Light of Clear Guidance
That He change notions, and set the scales of justice aright
And that He spread Love among you, O Muslims.

"Thus far the LORD has helped us."   1 Samuel 7:12b

FEBRUARY

"Forgive as the Lord forgave you."   Colossians 3:13b

"BLESSED are the poor in spirit,
    for theirs is the kingdom of heaven.
Blessed are those who mourn,
    for they will be comforted.
Blessed are the meek,
    for they will inherit the earth.
Blessed are those who hunger and thirst for righteousness,
    for they will be filled.
Blessed are the merciful,
    for they will be shown mercy.
Blessed are the pure in heart,
    for they will see God.
Blessed are the peacemakers,
    for they will be called children of God.
Blessed are those who are persecuted because of
righteousness,
    for theirs is the kingdom of heaven."

Matthew 5:3-10

"Love your enemies and pray for those who persecute you, that you may be children of your Father in heaven."

Matthew 5:44b-45a

"I can do everything through him who gives me strength."
Philippians 4:13 (NIV)

"Why, my soul, are you downcast? Why so disturbed within me? Put your hope in God, for I will yet praise him, my Saviour and my God."

Psalm 42:5

Scorch marks are still visible on the land outside Dogo Nahawa, Nigeria, which was the scene of anti-Christian violence in 2010

"Though the fig tree does not bud and there are no grapes on the vines, though the olive crop fails and the fields produce no food, though there are no sheep in the pen and no cattle in the stalls, yet I will rejoice in the LORD, I will be joyful in God my Saviour."
Habakkuk 3:17-18

"Those who hope in the LORD will renew their strength.
They will soar on wings like eagles; they will run and not
grow weary, they will walk and not be faint." Isaiah 40:31

When "Miriam's" beloved husband, a Christian pastor in a strict Muslim country, was stabbed to death, she was devastated and filled with hatred for their homeland. She said:

I felt as if I had mud in my hand and wanted to throw it at my enemies. One day a sister came to me and said, 'The Lord told me to tell you to pray for your enemies.' I replied that this was impossible for me. She continued, 'Just try – the Lord will give you the strength.'

So I began to pray – words spoken with my tongue, but without any meaning – 'Lord free me from this bondage of hatred and revenge.' After two or three days I felt my hand was empty of mud. This enabled me to start praying with sincerity for my enemies. I found that the hatred had gone, and in its place I began to feel love for my enemies. How beautiful it is to forgive. The Lord did this miracle for me, and now I am truly free.

> "Rejoice always, pray continually, give thanks in all circumstances; for this is God's will for you in Christ Jesus." 1 Thessalonians 5:16-18

Another lesson I had to learn was 1 Thessalonians 5:17-18 – 'in everything be thankful.' The Lord said to me, 'It is good you have forgiven. Now raise your hands and praise God.' I asked him, 'What for?' His reply was, 'Because I am reigning and have control of everything.' Thanking and praising were as difficult for me as forgiving had been, but in praising there was power. The Lord told me to start every day by praising. He said, 'Don't look at your situation, just at me.' So I learned to praise God every day in every situation. He enjoys our praises.

MARCH

"Consider it pure joy, my brothers and sisters, whenever you face trials of many kinds."

James 1:2

Ahmed Mustafa Abaza, from a prominent Egyptian Muslim family, knows what it means to suffer for Christ. After confessing his conversion to Christianity, he was beaten by his father who was trying to force him to return to Islam. Mr Abaza said:

> *My father despaired of me, because I would not change. He turned into a monster. He suspended me by chains; he tortured me with electricity and in other ways. But as he tried to kill my body, my soul was alive with Jesus, saying, 'Glory to the Lord'. Believe me, these torments, no matter how painful they were, I received with joy because He too – our Lord Jesus Christ – suffered for us.*

He was later taken to the Public Security Building where he suffered further beatings and torture for 17 months. Mr Abaza said:

> *Many of the prison guards became my friends when they understood what it means to be faithful to the truth despite increasing torture. They told me about hundreds, or maybe thousands, whom they had witnessed being tortured for the sake of Christ. During seventeen months in prison, Christ was my only companion. His closeness was sufficient to shorten this period for me despite my suffering. The prayers of the saints were my support. I felt the real presence of my Lord and was comforted.*

"Dear friends, do not be surprised at the fiery ordeal that has come on you to test you, as though something strange were happening to you. But rejoice inasmuch as you participate in the sufferings of Christ, so that you may be overjoyed when his glory is revealed."   1 Peter 4:12-13

"We were under great pressure, far beyond our ability to endure, so that we despaired of life itself... But this happened that we might not rely on ourselves but on God, who raises the dead."   2 Corinthians 1:8b,9b

Sudanese refugee children praying before a meal at a school
supported by Barnabas

"The prayers of the saints were my support."
Ahmed Mustafa Abaza

"But thanks be to God, who always leads us in triumphal procession in Christ and through us spreads everywhere the fragrance of the knowledge of him." 2 Corinthians 2:14 (NIV)

OUR Father in heaven,
We praise Your Name for the grace and courage You
grant to our brothers and sisters who suffer for their faith,
to those who endure poverty, hunger, discrimination
and mockery, to those who are beaten, imprisoned or
tortured, to those who have lost family and friends, home
and job, because of their decision to follow Jesus Christ
as Lord and Saviour.

Please fill them day by day with peace, joy and hope.
Give them a special awareness of Your loving presence
at all times. Strengthen them to endure hardship. Give
them Your words to say to those who despise and reject
them. Fill them with Your love for those who ill-treat
them and give them the grace to forgive and pray for their
persecutors.

We pray also for ourselves. Help us to remember that we
and they are members of one Body. Help us also to value
the freedom You have blessed us with and guide us to use
that freedom more wisely as we serve those who have
none, for their peace and to Your glory.
In Jesus' Name,

Amen

"The LORD's unfailing love surrounds those who trust in him."
Psalm 32:10b

APRIL

"Be still, and know that I am God."   Psalm 46:10a

"GOD is our refuge and strength,
    an ever-present help in trouble.
Therefore we will not fear, though the earth give way
    and the mountains fall into the heart of the sea,
though its waters roar and foam
    and the mountains quake with their surging.
There is a river whose streams make glad the city of God,
    the holy place where the Most High dwells.
God is within her, she will not fall;
    God will help her at break of day.
Nations are in uproar, kingdoms fall;
    he lifts his voice, the earth melts.
The LORD Almighty is with us;
    the God of Jacob is our fortress.
Come and see what the LORD has done,
    the desolations he has brought on the earth.
He makes wars cease to the ends of the earth;
    he breaks the bow and shatters the spear;
    he burns the shields with fire.
 'Be still, and know that I am God;
    I will be exalted among the nations,
    I will be exalted in the earth.'
The LORD Almighty is with us;
    the God of Jacob is our fortress."
                                      Psalm 46

"Whoever dwells in the shelter of the Most High will rest in the shadow of the Almighty. They will say of the LORD, 'He is my refuge and my fortress, my God, in whom I trust.'"

Psalm 91:1-2

"I lift up my eyes to the mountains – where does my help come from? My help comes from the LORD, the Maker of heaven and earth. He will not let your foot slip – he who watches over you will not slumber; indeed, he who watches over Israel will neither slumber nor sleep."

Psalm 121:1-4

"For you did not receive a spirit that makes you a slave again to fear, but you received the Spirit of sonship. And by him we cry, 'Abba, Father.' The Spirit himself testifies with our spirit that we are God's children." Romans 8:15-16 (NIV)

An elderly Pakistani woman who was the victim of a violent assault is comforted by a Barnabas partner from a Christian legal organisation

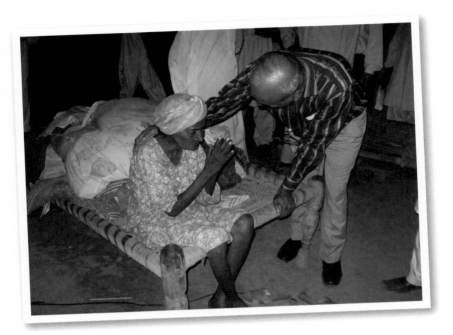

"I sought the LORD, and he answered me;
he delivered me from all my fears."
Psalm 34:4

"They cried out to the LORD in their trouble, and he delivered them from their distress."   Psalm 107:6

A couple of years after his conversion from Islam to Christianity, **Ali**, from Iran, gained the courage to tell his family about his new faith. Following the 1979 revolution, Iran became an Islamic Republic and religious freedom was severely limited with those who converted from Islam facing harassment, persecution, imprisonment and even death. In 1980 Iraq invaded Iran, triggering a bitter and bloody war that would last eight years. Against this background of oppression and danger, it was the peace and confidence of Christians that spoke most strongly to Ali's sister...

He said:

One evening, the movie 'Jesus' was to be shown at the church. My sister accompanied me to see the film. This was during the time that Iraqi jets bombed Tehran almost every night. During the middle of the film, as the bombing began and the anti-aircraft guns blasted, the lights went out. We sat in total darkness listening to the bombing and the blasts of the anti-aircraft guns. My sister leaned her head on my chest and began to cry. She insisted that we return home. However, no one else in the church left to look for shelter. Instead, everyone began to pray. Then a little candle was lit. I told my sister, 'If you find anyone else here who is fearful, we will go home.' As she looked around, she couldn't find a single frightened person. The pastor was standing in the front of the church praying. Soon, the electricity was restored and we were able to see the remainder of the movie. The startling events of that night caused my sister to become more interested in the life and teachings of Jesus Christ.

MAY

"I will fear no evil, for you are with me." Psalm 23:4b

After attending a Christian boarding school, 18-year-old Halima, from Nyasaland (now Malawi) decided to follow Christ and was baptised with the name **Maria Cecilia**. Her horrified Muslim father tried everything he could think of to bring her back to Islam, even calling in the mwaleem-mullah to "wash away" her Christianity with his rituals and incantations. A group of men were deputed to dig seven ditches and bring seven buckets of clean, cold water to pour over Maria who was dressed in a thin white kaftan and suffered the indignity of having her head shaved.

She described the ceremony:

The men who were to perform the cleansing ritual wore white outfits that made them look like the Ku Klux Klan. All I could see was the whites of their eyes, the rest of the eyes seemed red. I prayed that the Lord would not allow these devils with fiery eyes to touch me. They surrounded me and asked, 'Halima (my Muslim name), do you denounce and repent to your father Gulam and declare that you will give up Christianity?' My reply was, 'No!' spoken with calmness and serenity. I stopped shivering. I felt as if there were arms holding me up in a warm and comforting embrace. Then they poured a bucket of water over me to cleanse me of Christianity and my belief in Jesus Christ. They did this seven times, and each time I answered, 'No' in my native language

Chechewa. There was a murmur of Arabic prayers being said for my soul, the lost child of a family of strong Muslims. I was considered as good as dead.

After the ceremony my uncle intervened and said, 'This girl has seen something which we do not see. Gulam, let her go and I will care for her.' Apparently every time I said. 'Eeyayee!' ('no' in Chechewa) there had been a white cloud around me. Instead of anger my uncle had felt calm and peaceful. This feeling apparently spread right through the group including my father Gulam and the mwaleen who was pouring buckets of water over me, as I stood in each new ditch. By the end none of them was looking angrily at me. They could not understand how I underwent that ceremony and still emerged smiling. Of course, I did not do it alone. My faith and belief in Jesus Christ as the Son of God did it, praise the Lord!

Maria Cecilia eventually moved to Britain but returned to Malawi in 2003 when her 93-year-old mother was very sick. Maria's prayers for her mother's healing were answered, prompting the latter to follow Christ also. Many other family members have also become Christians.

Irrawaddy Delta, Burma (Myanmar), the area worst affected by
Cyclone Nargis in 2008

"When you pass through the waters, I will be with you;
and when you pass through the rivers, they will not sweep over you."
Isaiah 43:2a

"Be still before the LORD and wait patiently for him; do not fret when people succeed in their ways, when they carry out their wicked schemes." Psalm 37:7

"But you, LORD, are a shield around me, my glory, the one who lifts my head high."

I BIND unto myself today
The strong name of the Trinity,
By invocation of the same,
The Three in One, and One in Three.

Against the demon snares of sin,
The vice that gives temptation force,
The natural lusts that war within,
The hostile men that mar my course;
Or few or many, far or nigh,
In every place, and in all hours,
Against their fierce hostility,
I bind to me these holy powers.

Against all Satan's spells and wiles,
Against false words of heresy,
Against the knowledge that defiles,
Against the heart's idolatry,
Against the wizard's evil craft,
Against the death-wound and the burning,
The choking wave, the poisoned shaft.
Protect me Christ, till thy returning.

Extracts from St *Patrick's Breastplate*, a hymn traditionally attributed to
Patrick, who brought the Gospel to Ireland in the fifth century. It was written in
a context of persecution including both physical and spiritual opposition.

"There is no one like the God of Jeshurun, who rides on the heavens to help you and on the clouds in his majesty. The eternal God is your refuge, and underneath are the everlasting arms."
Deuteronomy 33:26-27a

42

"Do not be anxious about anything, but in every situation, by prayer and petition, with thanksgiving, present your requests to God. And the peace of God, which transcends all understanding, will guard your hearts and your minds in Christ Jesus." Philippians 4:6-7

JUNE

"There is no wisdom, no insight, no plan that can succeed against the LORD."   Proverbs 21:30

"Michael" converted from Islam to Christianity in Egypt after learning, through Christian friends, that it is God who seeks us – not the other way round. He was rejected by his Muslim family and friends, and later arrested and imprisoned by the secret police. Michael was beaten, tortured and held in solitary confinement for nine months.

After he had been declared insane and sent to a psychiatric clinic, where he was given electric shocks to his spine, the Mufti – the highest religious court – ordered that he must leave Islamic territory. Michael, who was in his mid-20s, faced the threat of death at the hands of Muslims as long as he remained in Egypt. He had to live in hiding, and suffered the devastating loss of his fiancée in an ambush shooting, before God provided an escape...

Eventually, completely exhausted, I was able to find safety in a desert monastery, where I could slowly recover physically and emotionally. An anonymous donor sent me an airline ticket and a European visa. I knew that departing from Cairo airport was dangerous, as my name was bound to have been 'blacklisted'. But there was no alternative. Trusting in God's help, I joined the queue at passport control. Just before I reached the desk, the computer crashed. In the ensuing chaos nothing on the database could be checked, but only the documents that each person was carrying. Mine were in order and I boarded the plane.

Since then I have lived in Europe and it is these words of Jesus that keep me going even here today: 'You did not choose me, but I chose you and appointed you so that you might go and bear fruit – fruit that will last.' (John 15:16) 99

"Though I walk in the midst of trouble, you preserve my life; you stretch out your hand against the anger of my foes, with your right hand you save me." Psalm 138:7

"Though he brings grief, he will show compassion, so great is his unfailing love. For he does not willingly bring affliction or grief to any human being." Lamentations 3:32-33

"Wait for the LORD; be strong and take heart and wait for the LORD."

Psalm 27:14

Barnabas pays for counselling to help reconcile children, abducted and brutalised by the Lord's Resistance Army in Uganda, with their parents

"Hold out your hand to them in friendship.
And you will then by God be blessed."
Chris Trigger

"Is anything too hard for the LORD?"

THE Son of Man in all His glory
Will sit upon His heavenly throne
"Let all the nations pass before Me,
I shall choose who are My own.

"You that fed Me when I hungered,
You that quenched My raging thirst:
You are My sheep, I am your Shepherd
You are the ones who shall be first.

"I was a stranger, and you healed Me;
I was naked; Me you clothed.
I was sick; you gave Me comfort;
A prisoner, and was not loathed."

Those righteous ones will then ask of Him,
"When did we do these things You say?"
The Son of Man will answer gently,
"You did these things for Me today.

"For when you tended to My brothers,
Cared for My sisters, friends, you see,
And did it for the least among them,
Then you did it as for Me."

So when, in times of tribulation,
Your brothers and sisters are oppressed,
Hold out your hand to them in friendship
And you will then by God be blessed.

The Son of Man in all His Glory by Barnabas supporter Chris Trigger, Devon, UK

JULY

"We must obey God rather than human beings." Acts 5:29b

WE think mocking, ridicule and scorn is persecution.
We have not yet faced prison, torture and execution.
We have not yet faced stones like Stephen.
Lord, help us to remember those in prison.

The gates of hell shall not prevail though it seems so strong.
Your eternal kingdom will come not too long,
And you will put right every wrong.
The whole earth will be filled with your song.

From Pharaoh to Nero there have been many persecutors.
Let us stand brave when facing our Nebuchadnezzars.
Our blood may be spilled like the many martyrs,
But oh may we have the faith of our fathers.

Extracts from *The Voice of the Martyrs* by Barnabas supporter Carlisle Clarke,
London, UK

"For our light and momentary troubles are achieving for us an eternal glory that far outweighs them all."

2 Corinthians 4:17

A child from North Korea, one of the worst places in the world for Christians

"For we know that if the earthly tent we live in is destroyed,
we have a building from God, an eternal house in heaven,
not built by human hands."
2 Corinthians 5:1

"The LORD is my light and my salvation – whom shall I fear? The LORD is the stronghold of my life – of whom shall I be afraid?"
Psalm 27:1

54

"When calamity comes, the wicked are brought down,
but even in death the righteous seek refuge in God."

Proverbs 14:32

Iranian evangelist **Mehdi Dibaj**, who had converted from Islam to Christianity in his late teens, was imprisoned when the country became an Islamic Republic following the 1979 Iranian Revolution. He endured nine years in prison where he faced torture and solitary confinement before eventually being brought to trial in 1993 – charged with apostasy from Islam. He was sentenced to death but released in January 1994 following an international outcry. He was kidnapped and killed in mysterious circumstances later that year.

In a written defence at his trial Mehdi Dibaj said:

I would rather have the whole world against me but know that the Almighty God is with me, be called an apostate but know that I have the approval of the God of glory... They tell me, 'Return!' But from the arms of my God to whom can I return? Is it right to accept what people are saying instead of obeying the Word of God? It is now 45 years that I am walking with the God of miracles, and His kindness upon me is like a shadow and I owe Him much for His fatherly love and concern.

The good and kind God reproves and punishes all those whom He loves. He tests them in preparation for heaven. The God of Daniel, who protected his friends in the fiery furnace, has protected me for nine years in prison and all the bad happenings have turned out for our good and gain, so much so that I am filled to overflowing with joy and thankfulness.

Therefore I am not only satisfied to be in prison for the honour of His Holy Name, but am ready to give my life for the sake of Jesus my Lord and enter His kingdom sooner, the place where the elect of God enter everlasting life, but the wicked to eternal damnation.

"Therefore I tell you, do not worry about your life, what you will eat or drink; or about your body, what you will wear. Is not life more important than food, and the body more important than clothes? ... See how the flowers of the field grow. They do not

labour or spin. Yet I tell you that not even Solomon in all his splendour was dressed like one of these. If that is how God clothes the grass of the field, which is here

today and tomorrow is thrown into the fire, will he not much more clothe you – you of little faith? So do not worry,

saying, 'What shall we eat?' or 'What shall we drink?' or 'What shall we wear?' For the pagans run after all these things, and your heavenly Father knows that you need them. But seek first his kingdom and his righteousness, and all these things will be given to you as well. Therefore do not worry about tomorrow, for tomorrow will worry about itself. Each day has enough trouble of its own."

Matthew 6:25, 28b-34

"My dear brothers and sisters, stand firm. Let nothing move you. Always give yourselves fully to the work of the Lord, because you know that your labour in the Lord is not in vain."

1 Corinthians 15:58

AUGUST

"For you alone, O LORD, make me dwell in safety."

Psalm 4:8b (NIV)

Egyptian lawyer and human rights' activist **Nagla Al-Imam** was detained, interrogated and beaten by security personnel after a peaceful demonstration of her Christian faith – carrying a cross and a coffin in front of a Cathedral – in defiance of the country's lack of religious freedom.

She described the treatment she received at the hands of her interrogator:

> He said, 'Yes my lady, why are you making trouble for us? Don't you want to be safe?' I said, 'It is you who do not want to be safe. You have restrained me from travelling, and I am a human rights' activist.' He said, 'Yes.' Then he went to take hold of the cross (on a chain around Nagla's neck) and asked, 'Who is this?'

> This time my words were harsh. I told him, 'Take your hands off the cross, for you don't know its worth.' He said, 'No, I know its worth.' He held the chain and tightened it around my neck. He was showing that he was threatening to cut the chain, or to hurt my neck, or do anything.

> Then I answered him. I said, 'If you touch me, I will react severely. If you are a real man, hit me.' He did not give me a

chance to complete the sentence. Holding my hair, he bashed my face against the desk. He slapped my face more than once, and punched me in the ribs, and on my arm. By this time I was bleeding from the side of my mouth.

I told him, 'Proceed with your documentation, if you have any.' He said, 'I don't have any documentation. I am just telling you this. This is just having fun. If you don't want to be safe, you will receive what you have not expected.'

I said, 'What is it that I could not expect? Will you put me in jail? So many other converts are in jail. You will kill me? So many converts have been killed.' I told him I was not afraid; 'I am not afraid because I know where I will be going, but what about you, who do not know where will you be going.'

Nagla was eventually allowed home where she reflected on her ordeal:

There is no safety – human safety, worldly safety – apart from the true safety I found with the Lord Jesus Christ. I am without work; threatened to be deregistered; without an income; without family. I have no one but enemies.

I felt this was God's discipline: He was teaching me what it means to be humble; what it means that the Lord will fight for you, and you shall hold your peace; what it means to focus my sight on Christ alone, and not to depend on human hands.

"To fear anyone will prove to be a snare, but whoever trusts in the Lord is kept safe."   Proverbs 29:25

"The LORD will fight for you; you need only to be still."

Exodus 14:14

Christians in Burma (Myanmar) find shelter after Cyclone Nargis, 2008

"There is no safety...apart from the true safety I found
with the Lord Jesus Christ."
Nagla Al-Imam

"My grace is sufficient for you, for my power is made perfect in weakness."

2 Corinthians 12:9a

YOU are the salt of the earth
Yet treated as scum
You are the conquerors supreme
Yet we see you beaten down
And pushed around
You are citizens of the Highest Kingdom
Yet here as third class
The lowest rung is where you rest.
You are seated in heavenly places
Yet here on damp dirty prison floors
You lay your head
You are so so loved by your Father
Yet here hatred and rejection
Is your lot
Except by us who love you and pray
For you
Take courage my brothers and sisters
And remember...
Who you are in Christ

Ode to the Persecuted Church by Barnabas supporter Lynne White, Hampshire, UK

SEPTEMBER

"For to me, to live is Christ and to die is gain." Philippians 1:21

WELL I know I spend a bit too much on clothes
And I must admit I care a bit too much about my hair
And it's true I eat my food for taste or comfort not for hunger
I am sorry that I live my life as if you were not there

When you, you wonder if you'll wake each day
And you, you gather secretly to pray
And you, you know that death's a part of living
And you are my sister and my brother
So maybe I could pray a little harder

A picture of you flashes through my mind
As I think about the way you live and die each day
But I am so comfortably removed from your situation
It is not hard to forget about the price you pay

You © Claire Hazzard 2008

"Truly my soul finds rest in God; my salvation comes from him. Truly he is my rock and my salvation; he is my fortress, I will never be shaken."   Psalm 62:1-2

"I have hidden your word in my heart that I might not sin against you."

Zimbabwean believers pray over the land after receiving training in Christian agricultural methods with help from Barnabas

"You are my sister and my brother."
Claire Hazzard

"I care very little if I am judged by you or by any human court; indeed, I do not even judge myself. My conscience is clear, but that does not make me innocent. It is the Lord who judges me."

1 Corinthians 4:3-4

Tahir Iqbal had an orthodox Muslim upbringing, and as a young man became an Islamic extremist. However a crippling attack of paralysis brought an early end to his career in the Pakistan Air Force and his family abandoned him. Left paraplegic, the only assistance Tahir received came from a local group of Christians who helped him acquire a wheelchair. He decided to study the Christian faith, and soon professed faith in Christ.

Tahir ran a small watch-repair business and witnessed openly to his customers, giving such convincing answers to the Muslims who enquired about his new faith that the imam could not counter them.

He was accused of blasphemy after the imam discovered Tahir had written notes in a copy of the Qur'an and was later sentenced to death for insulting the Holy Prophet.

While in jail, he was under constant pressure to renounce Christ, but he told his persecutors:

> *You want me to say that I changed my religion because somebody pushed me into it for the sake of money, to get a job, or to have women. But you are lying. You should know that I changed because I found the truth. I will kiss the rope that hangs me, but I will never deny my faith.*

Tahir died in suspicious circumstances in prison. Two weeks before his death in 1992, Tahir had told one of his friends who visited him:

> *I am ready to die and I am going to heaven where it will be better for me!*

"Do not let your hearts be troubled. Trust in God; trust also in me. My Father's house has plenty of room; if that were not so, would I have told you that I am going there to prepare a place for you? And if I go and prepare a place for you, I will come back and take you to be with me that you also may be where I am." John 14:1-3

OCTOBER

"If God is for us, who can be against us?"   Romans 8:31b

"Amy" from West Africa suffered years of persecution both in her homeland and later when her Muslim family moved to the UK. She had converted to Christianity aged 15 after her maths and science tutor, who was a Christian, introduced her to the gospel.

She said:

> *One day, I went to my room and prayed, desperate to know the truth. At first I prayed, 'Allah, Allah' but nothing happened. Then I tried saying, 'Jesus, Jesus.' I felt the glory of God fill the room and I began to sob. I went to my tutor and told him what had happened, and he helped me to receive Christ into my life. That was on 14 August 2001 when I was 15 years old. For the next year or so, I faced much opposition. My family is very large and includes many imams and sheikhs. They tried everything they could think of to force me back to Islam. They took me to a witch-doctor and to an Islamic teacher. They beat me and put potions in my food.*

Amy's sufferings intensified when she went to live with her parents in England in 2003. Her father took away her passport and beat her repeatedly over the next two years. He destroyed her college work and repeatedly threatened to kill her before throwing her out of the house – two days before her first A-Level exam. But nothing would deter her from getting baptised that summer.

Looking back in 2010, now married to the tutor who had led her to Christ, Amy said:

The Lord kept me through my sufferings in four ways: His peace that passes all understanding; His joy that does not depend on happenings; His hope that is assuring; and His Love that endures. As a Muslim I never knew Allah as my father but the father of our Lord Jesus is indeed a father to me.

The Lord has been my rock and knowing that my faith was based on a solid foundation I feared no harm. I can remember an incident when my grandmother took me to a 'marabout' (witchdoctor) and as soon as I entered his den he told her that I had a greater power protecting me. This was enough for me to be convinced that Jesus' power to protect his own was greater than any power in the entire universe. All through my suffering I felt the Lord's hand and protection. Sometimes when I was beaten up I felt no pain and this amazes me up to this day. ,,

"And he will be called Wonderful Counsellor, Mighty God, Everlasting Father, Prince of Peace. Of the increase of his government and peace there will be no end."

Isaiah 9:6b-7a

"For I am convinced that neither death nor life, neither angels nor demons, neither the present nor the future, nor any powers, neither height nor depth, nor anything else in all creation, will be able to separate us from the love of God that is in Christ Jesus our Lord."   Romans 8:38-39

Sunrise on the Kalahari desert border of South Africa and Botswana

"For the LORD God is a sun and shield."
Psalm 84:11a

"We know that all things work together for good for those who love God, who are called according to his purpose."

Romans 8:28 (NRSV)

HEAVENLY Father,
We lift up to You those who have to pay the price
for following You. May Your love and Your presence
surround them at all times. May they take heart
and be at peace because they know that You have
overcome the world. We thank You for their faith, that
despite persecution and hardship, they place their
trust in You. We pray that their faithfulness will inspire
us to follow You more closely and surrender all to
You.
In Jesus' precious Name,

Amen.

NOVEMBER

"What god will be able to rescue you?" Daniel 3:15b

"FURIOUS with rage, Nebuchadnezzar summoned Shadrach, Meshach and Abednego. So these men were brought before the king, and Nebuchadnezzar said to them, 'Is it true, Shadrach, Meshach and Abednego, that you do not serve my gods or worship the image of gold I have set up? Now when you hear the sound of the horn, flute, zither, lyre, harp, pipe and all kinds of music, if you are ready to fall down and worship the image I made, very good. But if you do not worship it, you will be thrown immediately into a blazing furnace. Then what god will be able to rescue you from my hand?' Shadrach, Meshach and Abednego replied to him, 'King Nebuchadnezzar, we do not need to defend ourselves before you in this matter. If the God we serve is able to deliver us, then he will deliver us from the blazing furnace and from Your Majesty's hand. But even if he does not, we want you to know, Your Majesty, that we will not serve your gods or worship the image of gold you have set up.'"

Daniel 3:13-18

"Call on me in the day of trouble; I will deliver you, and you will honour me." Psalm 50:15

"Summon your power, O God; show us your strength, O God, as you have done before." Psalm 68:28 (NIV)

Daniel chapter 3 in an Arabic Bible

"Who is Jesus? Is he the Son of God?
Is he the Saviour? How can we get eternal life?"
Iraqi prisoners of war

"Who can speak and have it happen if the Lord has not decreed it? Is it not from the mouth of the Most High that both calamities and good things come?" Lamentations 3:37-38

During the Iran-Iraq war in the 1980s, many soldiers fighting for Iraq were captured. During their time as prisoners of war (POWs), they were lectured by their Iranian captors on the subject of "only Muslims will be saved". A group of 36 Muslim prisoners began asking their lecturer for proof of this. The lecturer lost patience with their questions and accused them of being Christians masquerading as Muslims. He ordered them to be given a period of solitary confinement, with a regime of torture.

However, this harsh treatment simply stimulated their interest in Jesus. They managed to buy a Bible from an Iranian and they asked Christian Iraqi POWs to help them find answers in the Bible to their questions such as, "Who is Jesus? Is he the Son of God? Is he the Saviour? How can we get eternal life?"

When the Iranians discovered what these POWs were doing they lined up the 36 men and ordered whoever believed in Jesus to step forward. Courageously five did so. As they stood there silently testifying to their new found faith in Jesus, they were told that they would be hanged as apostates from Islam. However, that very day, the Iraqi government announced that for every Iraqi POW killed by the Iranians, Iraq would kill ten Iranian POWs. So, because of this threat, the Iranian authorities backed down and the converts were spared.

"LORD, there is no one like you to help the powerless against the mighty."

2 Chronicles 14:11b

DECEMBER

"Seek and you will find." Matthew 7:7b

Sharafuddin, from Malaysia, was schooled in a rigorous Islamic system but at university he found his routine religious practices unsatisfactory and began to question his Muslim faith.

He said:

> I discovered that God was very distant and far away from me. Muslims are expected to believe in things, blindly... It is no surprise at all that we as growing Muslims were soundly and regularly scolded, rebuked and punished for asking 'too many' questions about doubtful and dubious aspects of Islamic teachings. The typical response (from Islamic teachers) was, 'These are God's words, just believe it and obey it!' Later we found that they themselves were at a total loss, unable to handle and answer our honest questions with intelligence or logic! It was these experiences which contributed to the shattering of my confidence and conviction in the veracity of Islam and its teachings.

He began to study the works of non-Muslims to find out their views on life, including *Mere Christianity* by C.S. Lewis, which satisfied his search for answers and especially for spiritual truth. Around this time, Sharafuddin began to study the Christian Gospel.

He said:

I was finally drawn to one passage of Scripture, John 3:16.

"For God so loved the world that he gave his one and only Son, that whoever believes in him shall not perish but have eternal life." John 3:16

This is the true and real expression of the love of God, for me. How different from Islam's teaching of His 'love and mercy' – which actually cannot be known and understood! Today, my whole family and I have embraced the great blessings and guidance of God Himself.

"I no longer call you servants, because servants do not know their master's business. Instead, I have called you friends, for everything that I learned from my Father I have made known to you."   John 15:15

"Therefore, there is now no condemnation for those who are in Christ Jesus, because through Christ Jesus the law of the Spirit who gives life has set you free from the law of sin and death."

Romans 8:1-2

Indian Christian orphans of the 2004 tsunami celebrate Christmas

"If anyone is in Christ, the new creation has come:
The old has gone, the new is here!"
2 Corinthians 5:17

"Come to me, all you who are weary and burdened, and
I will give you rest. Take my yoke upon you and learn
from me, for I am gentle and humble in heart, and you
will find rest for your souls. For my yoke is easy and my
burden is light."

Matthew 11:28-30

"This is how God showed his love among us: He sent his one and only Son into the world that we might live through him. This is love: not that we loved God, but that he loved us and sent his Son as an atoning sacrifice for our sins."

1 John 4:9-10

GREAT is Your birth, Lord,
With a message of joy so deep,
A message of hope so high,
A message of love so wonderful,
A message of salvation so sure;
The message of a Father who loves, and Himself is love,
Who shows mercy, and Himself is mercy,
Your Father and ours, who call ourselves human beings.

But for You great is small, and small is great.
Human beings have passed You by these 2,000 years,
And have never really discovered love or mercy, joy or
hope,
Or the salvation they so desire, or even a Father
That gathers them together into one family,
And loved them before they came into being,
And loves them now in order to love them into eternity.

We may not understand this love.
But do not allow us to ignore or reject it.

Rt Rev Gabriel Zubeir Wako, Archbishop of Khartoum, Sudan

BARNABAS FUND/BARNABAS AID – WHO WE ARE

As part of the family of God, Barnabas Fund/Aid stands with our Christian brothers and sisters around the world, where they are in the minority and suffer discrimination, oppression and persecution as a result of their faith.

- We encourage prayer by Christians for their suffering brothers and sisters.
- We encourage donations from Christians and churches. Funds are channelled through local ministries and Christian organisations to bring about transformation in the lives of individual Christians and churches.
- We tell the untold story about the plight of persecuted Christians around the world. We also raise awareness about the challenge that Islam poses to the Church, its mission, and society.
- We speak out on behalf of Christians suffering injustice and violence, addressing religious and secular ideologies that deny full religious liberty to Christian minorities – while continuing to show God's love to all people.
- We witness to the love of Christ and building His Kingdom.

In love, through the grace of God, Barnabas Fund/Aid will stand for the truth. We seek to carry out our vision and purpose with compassion, integrity and grace, but we will not compromise what we believe the Word of God teaches.

Barnabas Fund/Aid works in over 60 countries:

- feeding an estimated 104,000 Christians in the last year
- educating over 5,000 children in 8 schools/educational programmes in 8 countries in the last 12 month
- supporting 279 evangelists and 126 pastors in 32 countries and working with 20 partner organisations in the past year
- helping to build and support 9 clinics and hospitals in 6 countries in the last 3 years
- providing 63,788 Bibles and Christian books in 16 languages to 14 different countries in the last year
- supporting Christians in 15 countries where there have been natural disasters and providing support for over 20,000 Christian families in these areas over the last 3 years
- training Christian leaders, providing help for victims of violence, enabling Christians to become self-sufficient, and supporting a range of other projects.

THE BARNABAS FUND/BARNABAS AID DISTINCTIVE

What helps make Barnabas Fund/ Aid distinctive from other Christian organisations that deal with persecution?

We work by:
- directing our aid only to Christians, although its benefits may not be exclusive to them ("As we have opportunity, let us do good to all people, *especially to those who belong to the family of believers."* Galatians 6:10, emphasis added)
- aiming the majority of our aid at Christians living in Muslim environments
- channelling money **from** Christians **through** Christians **to** Christians
- channelling money through existing structures in the countries where funds are sent (e.g. local churches or Christian organisations)
- using the money to fund projects that have been developed by local Christians in their own communities, countries or regions
- considering any request, however small
- acting as equal partners with the persecuted Church, whose leaders often help shape our overall direction
- acting on behalf of the persecuted Church, to be their voice – making their needs known to Christians around the world and the injustice of their persecution known to governments and international bodies.

We seek to:
- meet both practical and spiritual needs
- encourage, strengthen and enable the existing local Church and Christian communities – so they can maintain their presence and witness rather than setting up our own structures or sending out missionaries
- tackle persecution at its root by making known the aspects of the Islamic faith and other ideologies that result in injustice and oppression of non-believers
- inform and enable Christians in the West to respond to the growing challenge of Islam to Church, society and mission in their own countries
- facilitate global intercession for the persecuted Church by providing comprehensive prayer materials.

We believe:
- we are called to address both religious and secular ideologies that deny full religious liberty to Christian minorities – while continuing to show God's love to all people
- in the clear Biblical teaching that Christians should treat all people of all faiths with love and compassion, even those who seek to persecute them
- in the power of prayer to change people's lives and situations, either through grace to endure or through deliverance from suffering.